FRESH FRUIT DRINKS

Elegant, exotic and colorful — here is a wealth of mouth-watering drinks which are all as healthy as they are delicious.

By the same author
THE CAROB COOKBOOK
THE LITTLE BROWN BISCUIT BOOK

FRESH FRUIT DRINKS

by

Lorraine Whiteside

Color photography by the author
Line drawings by Ian Jones

THORSONS PUBLISHERS INC.
New York

Thorsons Publishers Inc.
377 Park Avenue South
New York, New York 10016

First U.S. Edition 1984

LIBRARY OF CONGRESS CATALOGING IN PUBLICATION DATA

Whiteside, Lorraine.
  Fresh fruit drinks.   —

   Includes index.
   ⌐1. Beverages.   2. Cookery (Fruit).   3. Fruit juices.
I. Title.
TX815.W45   1984   641.8'75   84-2429
ISBN 0-7225-0836-0 (pbk.)

Printed in Great Britain by Hazell Watson & Viney Limited,
Member of the BPCC Group, Aylesbury, Bucks

Thorsons Publishers Inc. are distributed to the trade by
Inner Traditions International Ltd., New York

CONTENTS

DEDICATION

I dedicate this book, with love
and thanks, to:

My beloved parents, Eric and Mary Whiteside,
for their devotion.

My treasured son, Daniel Satizábal,
for his love and inspiration.

INTRODUCTION

We are currently experiencing a revival of the cocktail era of the 1920's. We are also seeing, in this decade, a growing interest in natural foods and a widespread recognition of the important role of nutrition in ensuring a long, healthy and vigorous life. I like to think of this book as a representation of these two current vogues; a combination of the fun of creative cocktail making, coupled with an awareness of the long-term value of adequate daily nourishment.

Unfortunately, there still exists a mistaken assumption that healthy eating and healthy drinking are dull and lacking in imagination. I hope that this book can, in some small way, help put an end to this myth, for I believe that natural foods, and in particular fresh fruits, provide full scope for creativity and imaginative presentation.

The drinks included in this book contain only natural ingredients, yet they are colorful and appealing, and tempting to the taste buds. With such exotic and exciting names as El Dorado, Caribbean Dream, Isle of Capri and Waikiki Kiss, I feel sure that the label of dull and boring will not be applied to these beverages.

Vitamins and Minerals in a Glass
Part of the enjoyment of creating and preparing fruit drinks is knowing that they are as nutritious as they are delicious. Fresh fruits are storehouses of vital vitamins and minerals and have provided nourishment for mankind throughout the world since time immemorial. Fresh fruits are also an excellent source of unrefined carbohydrate, the substance that feeds our bodies with energy.

All the drinks included in this book contain one or more varieties of fruits or fruit juices. In some cases, the fruit is blended with other natural ingredients such as yogurt and milk, providing concentrated goodness in a glass. This type of fruit drink, because of its added protein, is ideal as an in-between-meals filler for children or as a dieter's meal-in-a-glass.

Creativity and Experimentation
Creating new blends of flavors, experimenting with color combinations and

trying out new methods of presentation and garnishing are part of the fun of cocktail making.

Unusual sunrise and sunset effects can be created with a delicious berry and honey purée. Drizzled over the drink and allowed to sink down to the bottom of the glass, a strawberry or raspberry purée will form red sunrise or sunset streaks through your cocktail. (This is particularly effective if the juice is poured over crushed ice, then drizzled with the red purée.) Egg white also adds an unusual and attractive appearance to fruit cocktails. It can either be blended with fruit juice, then allowed to separate from the juice and rise to the top of the glass, or hand-whisked, then spooned over the cocktail. (Illustrations of both these attractive effects are included in the book.) Remember also that egg white is full of protein and cholesterol-free, so not only are you adding appeal to your cocktails, you are adding nourishment as well. I also like to serve orange, melon and pineapple-based drinks in their respective shells — by using this method of presentation, a simple cocktail can be transformed into an exotic and irresistible delight.

This book provides just some of the ideas and methods that can be put into practice in creative cocktail making. I am sure that when confronted with a blender and a selection of fresh fruits, you will be able to create many tempting and nourishing drinks of your own.

Garnishing
Garnishing is an important aspect of cocktail presentation, based on the art of tempting the palate by appealing to the eye. Garnishes may be simple or elaborate, ranging from a small, fresh flower to a colorful array of fresh fruits. A particularly eye-catching garnish is prepared from a tuft of pineapple leaves left attached to the core. This is cut into quarters and formed into swizzle sticks. (The method is described fully in the book and an illustration is shown with Jamaican Fresco, page 37.)

A less exotic, yet equally appealing garnish is provided by using a sprig of fruit leaves, such as strawberry or raspberry, herb leaves, such as mint or thyme, or a colorful twist of citrus peel. Cherries and small paper parasols also add color to a cocktail. The type of garnish used is very much a matter of personal taste (and depends upon whatever happens to be available), but in all cases, the aim is to please the eye and tempt the palate.

Basic Equipment
The basic equipment required includes an electric blender, a citrus-fruit squeezer, a measuring cup, a nylon sieve and a grater.

The imagination and creative spirit must be provided by you. I am sure that you will enjoy the pleasure of making fruit drinks that are nourishing, full of flavor and immensely appealing. Good health!

Quantities given throughout the book are for one person.

1.
FRESH FRUIT
DRINKS

AEGEAN DAWN

Illustrated opposite.

The orange-pink flesh of the papaya is blended with milk, covered with wisps of snowy egg white and drizzled with a red purée of strawberry and honey in this irresistible cocktail.

½ small papaya
1 cup milk, chilled
Honey or raw cane sugar (optional)
½ egg white
2 strawberries
½ teaspoon clear honey (for purée)
Small flower

1. Peel and seed the papaya, then slice the flesh into a blender. Add the milk and blend until completely smooth. Add honey or sugar to taste, if desired, then blend again.

2. Pour the mixture into a tall glass.

3. Whisk the egg white until it stands in soft peaks, then spoon over the papaya-milk mixture, allowing the wisps of egg white to float on top.

4. Hull and rinse the strawberries, draining well. Press the strawberries through a nylon sieve, to purée. Add a little honey, blending well so that the honey is thoroughly absorbed. Just before serving, drizzle the strawberry-honey purée over the egg white. Garnish the drink with a small, exotic-looking flower. Serve accompanied by an iced-tea spoon.

Note: The papaya tree is popularly known in its native tropical America and West Indies as the "Medicine Tree". The papaya has gained its reputation as the "Fruit of Health" because of its highly-praised nutritive and medicinal properties. Rich in Vitamin A, the papaya also contains a powerful proteolytic enzyme known as papain. The enzyme's protein-digesting properties act as a valuable aid to digestion.

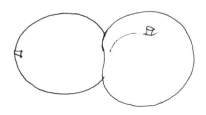

APPLE-BANANA YOGURT COCKTAIL

This creamy yogurt drink is made with a blend of apple, banana, natural yogurt and honey.

1 small, sweet dessert apple
½ banana, peeled and chopped
¾ cup plain yogurt, chilled
1-2 teaspoons clear honey
Apple slice
Sprig of fresh herb leaves

1. Peel and core the apple, then coarsely grate into a blender. Add the banana and yogurt and blend until completely smooth.

2. Add honey to taste and blend again.

3. Strain the liquid into a tall glass. Garnish with an apple slice and a sprig of fresh herb leaves.

Variations:
Apple-Pineapple Yogurt Cocktail. Substitute 2 tablespoons chopped pineapple for the banana. Proceed as above, adding a wedge of fresh pineapple to the garnish.
Apple-Strawberry Yogurt Cocktail. Substitute 4-6 strawberries for the banana. Proceed as above, adding a whole strawberry to the garnish.

APPLE-FRESH CURRANT COCKTAIL

Apple juice is blended with fresh currants and honey in this darkly delicious drink.

½ cup fresh currants, trimmed
1 cup apple juice, chilled
1-2 teaspoons clear honey
Apple slice
Blackcurrant or fresh herb leaves

1. Rinse the currants in a colander and drain well.

2. Place the fruit in a blender with the apple juice and blend until completely smooth. Add honey to taste and blend again.

3. Strain and pour into a tall glass. Garnish with an apple slice and a sprig of black currant or fresh herb leaves.

Variation:
Apple-Raspberry Cocktail. Substitute ⅔ cup raspberries for the black currants. Proceed as above, garnishing with raspberry or fresh herb leaves.

APPLE-NECTARINE MILK SHAKE

A two-fruit milk shake made with a blend of apple, nectarine and milk.

1 small, sweet dessert apple
1 small nectarine
1 cup milk, chilled
Honey or raw cane sugar (optional)
Apple slice
Sprig of fresh herb leaves

1. Peel and core the apple, then coarsely grate into a blender.

2. Blanch the nectarine in boiling water for about 30 seconds, then plunge into cold water. (The skin should slip off easily.) Peel, cut nectarine in half and discard the pit.

3. Slice the nectarine flesh into the blender with the apple. Add the milk and blend until completely smooth. Sweeten if desired and blend again.

4. Strain into a tall glass. Garnish with an apple slice and a sprig of fresh herb leaves.

Variations:
Apple-Pear Milk Shake. Substitute 1 small ripe pear, peeled and cored, for the nectarine. Blend with the apple and milk, adding 2 teaspoons fresh lemon juice. Sweeten if desired, garnish as above and top with a sprinkling of finely grated lemon zest.
Apple-Raspberry Milk Shake. Substitute ⅔ cup raspberries for the nectarine. Blend with the apple and milk; sweeten to taste if necessary. Strain and pour into a tall glass. Garnish with an apple slice, a few whole raspberries and a sprig of raspberry or fresh herb leaves.

ALMERIA COCKTAIL

Illustrated opposite.

A refreshing cocktail of white grape juice and fresh lime juice, served iced, with green grapes.

6-8 small, green seedless grapes
Juice of ½ lime
¾ cup white grape juice
Ice cubes

1. Rinse the grapes and place in a tall wine glass or Champagne flute.

2. Strain the lime juice and pour over the grapes.

3. Add the grape juice and stir thoroughly.

4. Add a few ice cubes and serve immediately, accompanied by an iced-tea spoon.

Variation:
Following the same procedure, substitute seeded bluish-black grapes, such as Concord or Ribier, fresh lime juice and red grape juice for the ingredients above. The juice of ½ lemon may be used instead of lime, if preferred.

As white and red grape juices are naturally sweet, the addition of fresh lime or lemon juice adds a tangy flavor to the beverage.

APPLE-ORANGE PUNCH

This thirst-quenching punch of apple, orange and lemon juices is served with chunks of diced apple and orange segments.

Juice of ½ lemon
½ cup apple juice, chilled
½ cup fresh orange juice, strained and chilled
Chunks of diced apple
Orange segments
Twist of orange peel

1. Strain the lemon juice into a tall glass, then add the apple and orange juices, stirring well.

2. Add chunks of diced apple and orange segments.

3. Garnish the fruit-laden punch with a colorful twist of orange peel and serve accompanied by an iced-tea spoon.

Variation:
For a slightly different blend of flavors, prepare the punch with apple juice, fresh mandarin orange juice and fresh lime juice. Add chunks of diced apple and mandarin orange segments. Garnish with a twist of lime peel.

APRICOT-ALMOND COCKTAIL

An irresistible cocktail of almond-flavored milk and fresh apricot.

1 large or 2 small apricots
1 cup almond milk, chilled (page 124)
Twist of orange peel

1. Blanch the apricot(s) in boiling water for about 30 seconds, then plunge into cold water. (The skin should slip off easily.) Peel, cut fruit in half and discard pits.

2. Slice the apricot flesh into a blender, add the almond milk and blend until smooth.

3. Pour into a tall glass. Garnish with a twist of orange peel.

Note: As almond milk has a naturally sweet taste, there should not be any need to add sugar or honey to this cocktail. However, if you do, take care not to over-sweeten, as this will destroy the delicate flavor.

APRICOT-MANGO YOGURT DRINK

Illustrated on page 18.

This blend of fresh apricot, mango, orange juice and natural yogurt makes a lusciously exotic and creamy beverage.

1 small apricot
½ small mango, peeled
6 tablespoons plain yogurt, chilled
6 tablespoons fresh orange juice, chilled
Honey or raw cane sugar (optional)
Orange slice
Cherry

1. Blanch the apricot in boiling water for about 30 seconds, then plunge into cold water. (The skin should slip off easily.) Peel, cut apricot in half and discard pit.

2. Slice the apricot flesh into a blender. Add the mango, yogurt and orange juice and blend until completely smooth. Taste and add a little honey or sugar, if desired, then blend again.

3. Strain the cocktail to remove any stringy bits of mango.

4. Pour into a tall glass. Garnish with a slice of orange and a cherry.

Variations:
Apricot-Nectarine Yogurt Drink. Substitute ½ nectarine for the mango. Blanch with the apricot, then proceed as above.
Apricot-Strawberry Yogurt Drink. Substitute 4 strawberries for the mango, and pineapple juice for the orange juice. Blend as above and garnish with a whole strawberry.

BALINESE SUNSET

Illustrated on page 19.

This combination of fresh orange juice and nectarine is poured over crushed ice and rippled with a deep red raspberry and honey purée, creating a sunset effect.

1 nectarine
¾ cup fresh orange juice
¼ cup raspberries
1 teaspoon clear honey
Crushed ice
Orange slice

1. Blanch the nectarine in boiling water for about 30 seconds, then plunge into cold water. (The skin should slip off easily.) Peel, cut fruit in half and discard pit.

2. Slice the nectarine flesh into a blender, add the orange juice and blend until completely smooth. Strain the mixture into a small bowl.

3. Hull the raspberries, rinse in a colander and drain well.

4. Press the raspberries through a nylon sieve to purée, then stir in the honey, blending thoroughly.

5. To serve, pour the nectarine-orange mixture into a tall glass filled with crushed ice. Slowly drizzle the raspberry-honey purée over the cocktail. As it sinks to the bottom of the glass, it will create red sunset streaks through the drink. Stir once very gently as the purée settles. Garnish with an orange slice.

Variation:
For a change, prepare the drink by blending the orange juice with peach, apricot, mango or papaya. Proceed as above.

For a simpler sunset cocktail, pour fresh orange juice over crushed ice, then streak with raspberry-honey purée, which will transform simple orange juice into an exotic delight.

APRICOT BLOSSOM

A flavorful blend of apricot, fresh orange juice and orange blossom honey.

1 large or 2 small apricots
¾ cup fresh orange juice, strained and chilled
1 teaspoon orange blossom honey
Twist of orange peel
Sprig of fresh herb leaves

1. Blanch the apricot(s) in boiling water for about 30 seconds, then plunge into cold water. (The skin should slip off easily.) Peel, cut fruit in half and discard pit(s).

2. Slice the apricot flesh into a blender, then add the orange juice and honey. Blend until completely smooth.

3. Pour into a tall glass. Garnish with a bright twist of orange peel and a contrasting sprig of fresh herb leaves.

Variations:
Peach or Nectarine Blossom. Prepare the drink as above, substituting a whole peach or nectarine for the apricot.
Apricot Yogurt Blossom. Decrease orange juice to ¼ cup. Add ½ cup natural yogurt and blend and garnish as above.

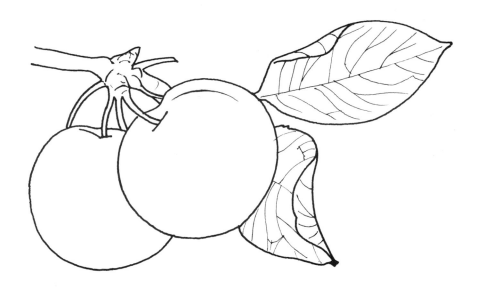

BOUGAINVILLAEA

Illustrated opposite.

This blend of strawberries, pineapple juice, egg white and honey creates a charming drink with contrasting layers — a deep pink base, topped with a delicately pale pink head.

6 strawberries
3/4 cup pineapple juice, chilled
1/2 egg white
1-2 teaspoons clear honey
Small pink or white flowers

1. Hull and rinse the strawberries, draining well.

2. Place the fruit in a blender with the pineapple juice, egg white and honey. Blend at high speed until creamy and frothy.

3. Strain the mixture into a tall glass and set aside for a minute or two to allow the egg white to separate from the juices and rise to the top. The deep pink blend of strawberries and pineapple juice will be topped with a pink-tinged froth.

4. Garnish with a few small pink or white flowers.

BUCK'S SPARKLE

This cooling combination of fresh orange juice and sparkling mineral water is served iced, with orange segments.

3/4 cup fresh orange juice
Ice cubes
Sparkling mineral water
Orange segments
Twist of orange peel
Small paper parasol

1. Strain the orange juice into a large glass.

2. Add ice cubes and fill with sparkling mineral water, stirring well.

3. Add orange segments and garnish with a bright twist of orange peel and a colorful paper parasol. Serve accompanied by an iced-tea spoon.

BANANA-MAPLE SHAKE

The unique flavor of pure maple syrup combines particularly well with this blend of banana and milk.

1 ripe banana
1 cup milk, chilled
1-2 teaspoons pure maple syrup
Finely grated orange zest
Twist of orange peel

1. Peel the banana and slice the flesh into a blender. Add milk and maple syrup and blend until smooth and creamy.

2. Pour into a tall glass and top with a sprinkling of finely grated orange zest. Garnish with a twist of orange peel.

Variation:
Banana-Apricot Maple Shake. Blanch 1 small apricot, peel and pit. Use only ½ banana, blending and garnishing as above.

BANANA, SOY AND HONEY SHAKE

A protein-packed and delicious blend of banana, soy milk, lemon juice and honey.

1 ripe banana
1 cup soy milk, chilled (page 126)
2 teaspoons fresh lemon juice
1-2 teaspoons clear honey
Finely grated lemon zest
Twist of lemon peel

1. Peel and slice the banana. Place in a blender with the soy milk, lemon juice and honey and blend until smooth and creamy.

2. Pour, unstrained, into a tall glass. To add some color, top with a sprinkling of finely grated lemon zest and garnish with a bright twist of lemon peel.

BELLA VISTA

This fruit-laden drink is rich with a blend of fresh strawberries, banana and pineapple juice.

6 strawberries
1/2 banana, peeled and sliced
3/4 cup pineapple juice, chilled
Strawberry or fresh herb leaves
Small paper parasol

1. Hull the strawberries, rinse in a colander and drain well. Set aside 2 strawberries for garnishing.
2. Place the remaining strawberries in a blender with the banana and the pineapple juice and blend until completely smooth.
3. Strain the mixture to remove the strawberry seeds.
4. Pour into a large stemmed glass and garnish with the reserved strawberries and a sprig of strawberry or fresh herb leaves. Complete the garnish by adding a colorful paper parasol.

CALIFORNIA DREAM

Illustrated opposite.

This blend of pink grapefruit juice and fresh orange juice is topped with a snowy white head.

6 tablespoons red grapefruit juice, strained and chilled
6 tablespoons fresh orange juice, strained and chilled
1/2 egg white

1. Pour the chilled juices into a blender and add the egg white. Blend at high speed until mixture is frothy.
2. Pour into a tall tumbler, then leave to stand for a few minutes before serving. The egg white will separate from the juices and rise to the top of the glass, creating a lovely snowy head.

Note: If pink grapefruit juice is unavailable, use ordinary grapefruit juice.

CAMOMILE FRUIT PUNCH

A soothing and refreshing punch made with camomile tea and pineapple juice, served with chunks of fresh pineapple and strawberries.

1/2 cup camomile tea, chilled
1/2 cup pineapple juice, chilled
Chunks of fresh pineapple
Sliced strawberries
Orange slice
Sprig of mint or fresh herb leaves

1. Mix the camomile tea and pineapple juice in a tall glass.
2. Add chunks of fresh pineapple and sliced strawberries.
3. Garnish with a slice of orange and a sprig of fresh mint or other fresh herb leaves. Serve accompanied by an iced-tea spoon.

Note: For variation, prepare the Camomile Fruit Punch with fresh orange juice, white grape juice or grapefruit juice, using equal proportions of the herbal tea and the chosen fruit juice. Add any of your favorite seasonal fresh fruits.

BERMUDA ROSE

Fresh strawberries, red grape juice, natural yogurt and honey are combined to make this crimson-pink drink.

6 strawberries
¾ cup red grape juice, chilled
1-2 teaspoons clear honey
1 tablespoon plain yogurt, chilled
Small pink or white flowers

1. Hull the strawberries, rinse in a colander and drain well.

2. Place the fruit in a blender, adding the grape juice, honey and yogurt. Blend until completely smooth.

3. Strain the mixture to remove the strawberry seeds.

4. Pour into a tall glass and garnish with a few small pink or white flowers.

BLACK MAGIC

A magical blend of black currants, natural yogurt, milk and honey is contained in this creamy, flavor-rich drink.

½ cup trimmed black currants
½ cup plain yogurt, chilled
¼ cup milk, chilled
1-2 teaspoons clear honey
Black currant or fresh herb leaves
Small flower

1. Rinse the currants in a colander and drain well.

2. Place the fruit in a blender with the yogurt and milk, blending until smooth and creamy. Add honey to taste, then blend again.

3. Strain the mixture and pour into a tall glass.

4. Serve garnished with a sprig of black currant or fresh herb leaves and a small, deep pink or white flower.

Variation:
Follow the same procedure as above, substituting blackberries for the black currants.

CANARIES FLIP

A nutritious blend of banana, egg, milk and honey creates a creamy drink.

1 small or ½ large banana
1 egg
1 cup milk, chilled
1 teaspoon clear honey
Freshly grated nutmeg
Small flowers

1. Peel the banana, slice the flesh into a blender and add the egg, milk and honey. Blend until completely smooth and creamy.

2. Pour the liquid into a tall glass and top with a sprinkling of freshly grated nutmeg. To add some color, garnish with a few small, brightly-colored flowers.

CARIBBEAN DREAM

Illustrated opposite.

This tempting combination of fresh pineapple, banana, milk and cream is served over crushed ice.

3 tablespoons chopped pineapple
½ small banana, peeled and chopped
¾ cup milk, chilled
3 tablespoons light cream
Honey or raw cane sugar (optional)
Crushed ice
Slice of fresh pineapple
Cherries

1. Place the pineapple, banana, milk and cream in a blender and blend until smooth. Taste and sweeten, if you wish, with a little honey or sugar and blend again.

2. Place plenty of crushed ice in a balloon glass and strain the mixture over the ice.

3. Peel and neatly core the slice of fresh pineapple and place over the rim of the glass. Position 2 straws through the center of the pineapple and add a few cherries to garnish.

CHAMPS ELYSEES

A mixture of pineapple juice and orange juice is poured over crushed ice, garnished with fresh peach and rippled with a raspberry and honey purée to create this eye-catching drink.

¼ cup raspberries
1 teaspoon clear honey
Crushed ice
½ peach, peeled and quartered
¼ cup pineapple juice, chilled
¼ cup fresh orange juice, strained and chilled

1. First prepare the raspberry-honey purée. Hull the raspberries, rinse in a colander and drain well.

2. Press the raspberries through a nylon sieve to purée. Stir the honey into the purée, blending well. Set aside.

3. Fill a large martini glass with crushed ice.

4. Place the peach segments in the glass, embedding between the sides of the glass and the ice, with the tops of the peaches hanging slightly over the rim of the glass.

5. Mix the juices together and pour over the crushed ice.

6. Slowly drizzle the prepared raspberry-honey purée over the juice mixture, allowing the purée to sink down to the bottom of the glass creating a rippled effect through the drink. Stir once very gently as the purée settles. Serve accompanied by an iced-tea spoon.

Note: This drink may be garnished with segments of fresh nectarine, if preferred.

CLOUD NINE

Nectarine, apricot and pineapple juice are combined to make this dreamy beverage.

1 small or ½ large nectarine
1 small or ½ large apricot
¾ cup pineapple juice, chilled
Honey or raw cane sugar (optional)
Twist of orange peel
Cherries

1. Blanch the nectarine and apricot in boiling water for about 30 seconds, then plunge into cold water. (The skins should slip off easily.) Peel, cut fruit in half and discard pits.

2. Slice the nectarine and apricot flesh into a blender, add the pineapple juice and blend until completely smooth. Add honey or sugar to taste, if desired, then blend again.

3. Pour into a tall glass and serve garnished with a colorful twist of orange peel and a few cherries.

Variation:
Substitute fresh orange juice for the pineapple juice, if preferred, or use equal proportions of pineapple and orange juices, blended with the nectarine and apricot as above.

CONFERENCE CUP

A harmonious blend of juicy pear and almond milk, with the added tang of fresh lemon juice and lemon zest.

1 small Anjou or other variety of pear
3/4 cup almond milk, chilled (page 124)
2 teaspoons fresh lemon juice
Honey or raw cane sugar (optional)
Finely grated lemon zest
Twist of lemon peel

1. Pare and core the pear, then slice the flesh into a blender.

2. Add the almond milk and fresh lemon juice and blend until completely smooth and creamy. Add honey or sugar to taste, if desired, then blend again.

3. Pour into a tall glass and top with a sprinkling of finely grated lemon zest. Garnish with a colorful twist of lemon peel.

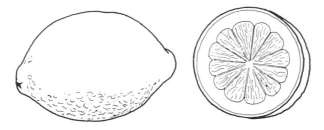

COPACABANA COCONUT

Illustrated opposite.

This exotic blend of coconut milk, papaya and lime juice is served in a coconut shell.

½ small papaya
¾ cup coconut milk, chilled (page 124)
1 teaspoon fresh lime juice
Vanilla sugar (page 58) or honey
Coconut shell
Cherries
Small paper parasol

1. Peel and seed the papaya, then slice the flesh into a blender.

2. Add the coconut milk and lime juice and blend until smooth. Add vanilla sugar or honey to taste and blend again.

3. Serve in the coconut shell or a tall cocktail glass, garnished with a few cherries and a small paper parasol. (If preferred, fill the coconut shell or cocktail glass with crushed ice, then pour in the blended drink.)

GUADALAJARA

This irresistibly fruity drink is made with a blend of mandarin orange juice, pineapple juice and banana.

²/₃ cup fresh mandarin orange juice, strained and chilled
6 tablespoons pineapple juice, chilled
1 small banana, peeled and chopped
Twist of mandarin orange peel
Small paper parasol

1. Place the mandarin orange juice, pineapple juice and banana in a blender and blend until completely smooth and creamy.

2. Pour mixture into a tall glass. Garnish with a twist of mandarin orange peel and a small, brightly-colored paper parasol.

EVENING SUN

This golden-yellow blend of fragrant nectarine and fresh orange juice is poured over crushed ice and topped with a rosy layer of fresh strawberries.

1 nectarine
¾ cup fresh orange juice, strained and chilled
Honey or raw cane sugar (optional)
Crushed ice
3-4 small strawberries, hulled and rinsed
Small yellow or white flowers

1. Blanch the nectarine in boiling water for about 30 seconds, then plunge into cold water. (The skin should slip off easily.) Peel, cut nectarine in half and discard pit.

2. Slice the nectarine flesh into a blender, add the orange juice and blend until smooth. Taste after blending, and if you wish to sweeten, add a little honey or sugar, then blend again.

3. Pack a tall glass with crushed ice and pour the blended mixture over the ice.

4. Slice the strawberries in half and place, cut side down, on top of the ice, forming a rosy layer against the golden-yellow liquid. Garnish with a few small yellow or white flowers and serve accompanied by an iced-teaspoon.

HAWAII BEACH

A long, refreshing drink of pineapple juice and sparkling mineral water, served iced, with chunks of fresh pineapple and cucumber slices.

¾ cup pineapple juice
Ice cubes
Sparkling mineral water
Chunks of fresh pineapple
Slices of cucumber
Pineapple core swizzle stick (see below)
Spiral of cucumber peel

1. Pour the pineapple juice into a tall glass, add ice cubes and fill with sparkling mineral water, stirring well.

2. Add chunks of fresh pineapple and slices of cucumber.

3. Garnish with a pineapple core swizzle stick and a long spiral of cucumber peel. Serve accompanied by an iced-teaspoon.

Note: To make *Pineapple Core Swizzle Sticks,* slice a whole pineapple in half, cutting lengthwise through the leaves. Slice each half into quarters, again cutting through the leaves. Cut the pineapple flesh away from the center core on each quarter, leaving a strip of core attached to each bunch of leaves. Trim the leaves, discarding any withered ones and shape the strip of core into an appropriately-sized swizzle stick. These swizzle sticks make an attractive and exotic garnish for fruit drinks, so always reserve the leaves and core to use when serving long drinks containing fresh pineapple.

EL DORADO

Illustrated opposite.

A golden blend of mango, orange juice and pineapple juice is topped with snowy egg white and drizzled with a raspberry and honey purée in this deliciously exotic and colorful cocktail.

½ small mango
6 tablespoons fresh orange juice, chilled
6 tablespoons pineapple juice, chilled
Honey or raw cane sugar (optional)
2 tablespoons raspberries
½ teaspoon clear honey (for purée)
½ egg white

1. Peel the mango and slice the flesh into a blender. Add the orange and pineapple juices and blend until smooth. Taste, and if necessary, sweeten with a little honey or sugar, then blend again.

2. Strain the mixture to remove the stringy bits of mango, then pour into a tall glass.

3. Hull and rinse the raspberries, draining well. Press the raspberries through a nylon sieve to purée. Add a little honey, blending well, so that honey is thoroughly absorbed.

4. Whisk the egg white until it stands in soft peaks, then spoon it over the liquid in the glass. Just before serving, drizzle with raspberry-honey purée.

Note: For variation, substitute peach, nectarine or apricot for the mango, blend with the two juices as above, top with the beaten egg white and drizzle with raspberry-honey purée.

HIGHLAND GLEN

This truly Scottish cocktail is made with a blend of flavorful oat milk and fresh raspberries.

²/₃ cup raspberries
1 cup oat milk, chilled (page 125)
Raspberry or fresh herb leaves

1. Hull the raspberries, rinse in a colander and drain well. Reserve 2 or 3 for garnish.
2. Place the remaining raspberries in a blender with the oat milk. Blend until smooth.
3. Strain mixture into a tall glass. Garnish with the reserved raspberries and a contrasting sprig of raspberry or fresh herb leaves.

HONEYDEW COBBLER

A delicious blend of honeydew melon and milk, served with honeydew melon balls.

¹/₃ cup diced Honeydew melon
1 cup milk, chilled
4-6 Honeydew melon balls
Sprig of fresh herb leaves
Small yellow flowers

1. Place the diced melon and milk in a blender and blend thoroughly until completely smooth.
2. Using a melon baller, shape some honeydew melon flesh into neat balls.
3. Pour the melon-milk mixture into a tall glass and add the melon balls.
4. Garnish with a sprig of fresh herb leaves and a few small yellow flowers. Serve accompanied by an iced-teaspoon.

Variations:
Honeydew-Banana Cobbler. Omit the melon balls. Add banana slices and garnish as above.

Honeydew-Pineapple Cobbler. Replace the melon balls with chunks of fresh pineapple. Garnish with a wedge of fresh pineapple and a few brightly-colored flowers.

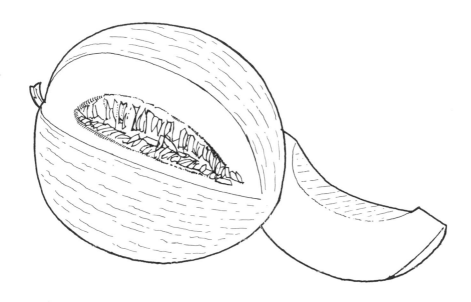

ICY LEMON AND HONEY COCKTAIL

This iced mixture of fresh lemon juice, honey and mineral water is cooling and refreshing.

Juice of 1 lemon
1 cup mineral water
1-2 teaspoons clear honey
Ice cubes
Twist of lemon peel

1. Strain the lemon juice into a tall glass.

2. Add the mineral water and honey, stirring well so that the honey is thoroughly blended.

3. Add ice cubes and garnish with a twist of lemon peel.

EXOTIC SPARKLER

Illustrated opposite.

Sparkling white grape juice and fresh lime juice are joined with exotic fruits.

Juice of ½ lime
¾ cup sparkling white grape juice, chilled
Chunks of fresh pineapple and mango
Slice of orange
Slice of kiwi fruit
Small paper parasol.

1. Strain the lime juice into a shallow Champagne or cocktail glass.

2. Add the sparkling grape juice, stirring well.

3. Add chunks of fresh pineapple and mango. Garnish with a slice of orange and kiwi fruit. Complete the garnish with a small paper parasol. Serve accompanied by an iced-tea spoon.

Variation:
Serve the cocktail with chunks of papaya, banana slices, peach, apricot or nectarine chunks, black or green seedless grapes, or any of your favorite exotic fruits.

ISLE OF CAPRI

Illustrated on page 117.

Fresh strawberries are blended with white grape juice, covered with folds of snowy egg white and drizzled with strawberry and honey purée in this romantic medley.

8 strawberries
¾ cup white grape juice, chilled
Honey or raw cane sugar (optional)
½ egg white
½ teaspoon clear honey
Small flower

1. Hull and rinse the strawberries, draining well. Set aside 2 strawberries for the purée.

2. Place the remaining strawberries in a blender with the grape juice and blend until smooth. Taste, and sweeten if you wish, with a little honey or sugar, then blend again.

3. Strain mixture to remove the strawberry seeds and pour into a tall, stemmed glass.

4. Whisk the egg white until it stands in soft peaks, then spoon over the blended strawberries and grape juice, allowing the egg white to float on top of the liquid.

5. Press the reserved strawberries through a nylon sieve to purée. Add the honey, blending well so that the honey is thoroughly absorbed.

6. Just before serving, drizzle the strawberry-honey purée over the egg white. Add a small, exotic-looking flower. Serve accompanied by an iced-tea spoon.

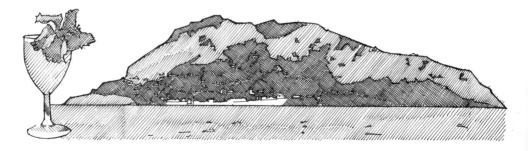

ITALIAN BEAUTY

An exquisite blend of cantaloupe melon and almond-flavored milk, served with fresh strawberries.

½ small Cantaloupe melon
1 cup almond milk (page 124)
4 strawberries
Small flowers

1. Peel and seed the cantaloupe, then slice into a blender.

2. Add the almond milk and blend thoroughly until completely smooth.

3. Pour the mixture into a tall glass.

4. Hull and rinse the strawberries, reserving one for the garnish. Slice the remaining strawberries and add them to the cocktail.

5. Garnish with the reserved strawberry and a few small, brightly-colored flowers.

Note: The true cantaloupe melon takes its name from the Italian estate of Cantalupo, near Rome, where it was first cultivated in the seventeenth century. With its fragrant, pinkish-orange, sweet and juicy flesh, it is one of the most succulent of melons. The somewhat similar melon known as cantaloupe in the United States is the netted muskmelon.

HONEYMOON

Illustrated opposite.

A lusciously fragrant blend of passion fruit, peach and fresh orange juice.

1 passion fruit
¾ cup fresh orange juice, chilled
1 small peach
Cherry

1. Cut the passion fruit in half and scoop out the seedy pulp with a spoon.

2. Place the passion fruit pulp in a nylon sieve, then strain the orange juice through the sieve, over the pulp, pressing the passion fruit seeds with the back of a spoon, making sure that the fruit juice and pulp are separated from the seeds. Repeat the straining process several times to ensure that the full flavor of the passion fruit is contained in the orange juice, with only bare black seeds remaining in the sieve. Discard the seeds.

3. Blanch the peach in boiling water for about 30 seconds, then plunge into cold water. (The skin should slip off easily.) Peel, cut the peach in half and discard pit.

4. Slice the peach flesh into a blender. Add the orange-passion fruit juice and blend until smooth.

5. Pour into a long-stemmed glass and serve garnished with a cherry.

Note: Passion fruit is the edible fruit of a particular species of the passion flower (Passiflora Edulis). It is grown in tropical regions throughout the world, particularly the West Indies, South America, parts of North America and North Africa. Passion fruit has a hard, wrinkled, brown skin and an edible, seedy pulp that is delightfully fragrant with a delicious and distinctive flavor. In tropical countries, the seedy pulp is scooped out and eaten with a spoon for refreshment. Add the pulpy juice of this fruit to a fresh fruit cocktail and the resultant flavor is magnificently exotic.

LEMON AND HONEY FLIP

A nutritious, creamy blend of lemon juice, honey, milk and egg.

Juice of ½ lemon
1 cup milk, chilled
1 egg
1-2 teaspoons clear honey
Twist of lemon peel

1. Strain the lemon juice into a blender.

2. Add the milk, egg and honey and blend until smooth.

3. Pour into a tall glass. Garnish with a bright twist of lemon peel.

LIME AND HONEY HIGHBALL

Fresh lime juice is blended with sparkling mineral water and honey for a refreshingly tangy taste.

Juice of 1 lime
Sparkling mineral water, chilled
1-2 teaspoons clear honey
Ice cubes
Twist of lime peel

1. Strain the lime juice into a highball glass.

2. Fill with sparkling mineral water.

3. Add honey to taste, stirring well so that the honey is completely absorbed.

4. Add the ice cubes and garnish with a deep green twist of lime.

Variation:
Lime Blossom Highball. Substitute lime blossom honey for the clear honey and proceed as above.

ORANGE AND NECTARINE YOGURT DRINK

Whole nectarine, fresh orange juice and natural yogurt are blended together in this lusciously creamy beverage.

1 nectarine
6 tablespoons fresh orange juice, strained and chilled
6 tablespoons plain yogurt, chilled
Honey or raw cane sugar (optional)
Orange slice
Cherry

1. Blanch the nectarine in boiling water for about 30 seconds, then plunge into cold water. (The skin should slip off easily.) Peel, cut in half and discard pit.

2. Slice the nectarine flesh into a blender, add the orange juice and yogurt and blend until completely smooth. Taste and add a little honey or sugar to sweeten, if you wish, then blend again.

3. Serve in a tall glass, garnished with a slice of orange and a cherry.

Variation:
Pineapple-nectarine Yogurt Cocktail. Substitute pineapple juice for the orange juice and proceed as above.

JADE

An unusual fruit and vegetable drink, rich in color and flavor, made with a blend of pineapple juice and watercress.

6-8 sprigs of watercress (or to taste)
1 cup pineapple juice, chilled

1. Trim and rinse the watercress. Reserve one sprig for garnish.
2. Place the remaining watercress in a blender with the pineapple juice and blend until the watercress is completely pulverized.
3. Strain the mixture into a tall glass. Garnish with the reserved sprig of watercress.

JAMAICAN FRESCO

Illustrated opposite.

A refreshing mixture of pineapple juice, orange juice and pink grapefruit juice, served with chunks of fresh pineapple and exotically garnished with pineapple leaves.

6 tablespoons pineapple juice, chilled
6 tablespoons fresh orange juice, chilled
6 tablespoons pink grapefruit juice, chilled
Ice cubes
Chunks of fresh pineapple
Orange slices
Pineapple core swizzle stick (page 37)

1. Combine the pineapple, orange and grapefruit juices.
2. Place plenty of ice cubes in a tall glass and strain the mixed juices over the ice.
3. Add chunks of fresh pineapple and garnish with orange slices and a pineapple core swizzle stick. Serve immediately, accompanied by an iced-tea spoon.

MANDARIN-LIME FRAPPE

Two exotic fruit juices, mandarin and lime, are combined and poured over crushed ice in this refreshing, rich-flavored frappé.

Juice of 1 lime
¾ cup fresh mandarin orange juice
Crushed ice
Twist of lime peel

1. Combine the lime and mandarin orange juices.

2. Fill a large cocktail glass with crushed ice, then strain the mixed juice over the ice.

3. Garnish with a twist of lime.

Variation:
Mandarin-Peach Frappé. Omit lime juice. Blanch 1 small peach in boiling water for about 30 seconds, then plunge into cold water. (The skin should slip off easily.) Peel, cut peach in half and discard pit. Slice peach flesh into a blender, add ¾ cup fresh mandarin orange juice and blend until smooth. Fill a large cocktail glass with crushed ice, strain contents of blender over the ice and garnish with a twist of mandarin orange peel.

MANGO-ORANGE FRAPPE

This blend of exotic mango and fresh orange juice, poured over crushed ice, is irresistibly luscious.

1/2 small mango
3/4 cup fresh orange juice
Crushed ice
Twist of orange peel

1. Peel the mango and reserve two small chunks for the garnish.

2. Slice the remaining mango into a blender, add the orange juice and blend until smooth. Strain through a nylon sieve to remove the stringy bits of mango.

3. Place plenty of crushed ice in a large cocktail glass and pour the mango-orange mixture over the ice.

4. Spear the reserved chunks of mango on a toothpick and use to garnish. Complete the garnish by adding a twist of orange peel.

Variation:
Mango-Pineapple Frappé. Substitute pineapple juice for the orange juice. Proceed as above.

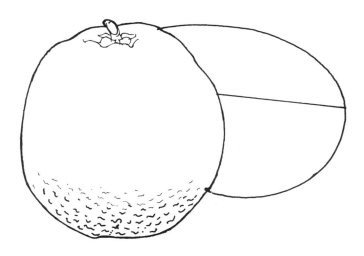

MANGO-LEMON COOLER

Illustrated opposite.

The deep-orange colored flesh of the exotic mango is blended with lemon juice and sparkling mineral water in this cooling drink.

1 small or ½ large ripe mango
Juice of ½ lemon
Sparkling mineral water or club soda, chilled
Honey or raw cane sugar (optional)
Slice of lemon

1. Peel the mango and slice the flesh into a blender. If using a whole mango, squeeze the pit with your hands to make sure that all the juice is extracted from any flesh remaining on the pit.

2. Add the lemon juice and blend well to reduce fruit to a purée.

3. Strain the purée through a nylon sieve to remove any stringy bits of mango. (Alternatively, dice the mango flesh into small chunks, combine with the lemon juice, mash to a purée with a fork, then press the purée through a nylon sieve.)

4. Place the mango-lemon purée in a tall glass and fill with sparkling mineral water or soda water, stirring well. Taste and sweeten with a little honey or sugar, if you wish, and stir thoroughly, so that honey or sugar is completely absorbed.

5. Garnish with a slice of lemon.

Variation:
Mango-Lime Cooler. Substitute the juice of ½ lime for the lime juice and proceed as above. Garnish with a slice of lime.

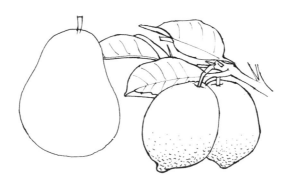

MOULIN ROUGE

A blend of rich red raspberries, pineapple juice, natural yogurt and honey is contained in this creamy, colorful drink.

2/3 cup raspberries
6 tablespoons pineapple juice, chilled
6 tablespoons plain yogurt, chilled
1-2 teaspoons clear honey
Small, deep-pink flowers

1. Hull the raspberries and rinse in a colander, draining well.

2. Place the raspberries in a blender with the pineapple juice and yogurt, blending until smooth and creamy. Sweeten with honey to taste, then blend again.

3. Strain the mixture to remove the raspberry seeds and pour into a tall, stemmed glass. Add a garnish of small, deep-pink flowers to enhance the color of the drink.

Variation:
Substitute white grape juice or orange juice for the pineapple juice and proceed as above.

NECTARINE-RASPBERRY MILK SHAKE

Raspberries and milk are blended with juicy, fresh nectarine in this richly flavored, two-fruit milk shake.

1 small or 1/2 large nectarine
1/2 cup raspberries
1 cup milk, chilled
Honey or raw cane sugar (optional)
Raspberry or fresh herb leaves

1. Blanch the nectarine in boiling water for about 30 seconds, then plunge into cold water. (The skin should slip off easily.) Peel, cut in half and discard pit. Slice the nectarine flesh into a blender.

2. Hull the raspberries, rinse in a colander and drain well. Reserve 2 raspberries for the garnish and place the remainder in the blender.

3. Add the milk and blend until completely smooth. Taste and sweeten with a little honey or sugar, if you wish, then blend again.

4. Strain the mixture to remove the raspberry seeds, then pour into a tall glass.

5. Garnish the milk shake with the reserved raspberries and a sprig of raspberry or fresh herb leaves.

Variation:
Nectarine-Strawberry Milk Shake. Substitute 4-6 strawberries for the raspberries. Proceed as above, garnishing with a whole strawberry and a sprig of strawberry or fresh herb leaves.

ORANGE AND GRAPEFRUIT PUNCH

A refreshing, tangy punch made with fresh orange juice and grapefruit juice, served with orange and grapefruit segments.

½ cup fresh orange juice, strained and chilled
½ cup grapefruit juice, strained and chilled
Orange and grapefruit segments
Sprig of mint or fresh herb leaves
Twist of orange peel

1. Combine the orange and grapefruit juices in a tall glass, stirring well.

2. Add a few orange and grapefruit segments to the glass and garnish with a sprig of mint or fresh herb leaves and a colorful twist of orange peel. Serve accompanied by an iced-tea spoon.

Variation:
Orange and Pineapple Punch. Substitute pineapple juice for the grapefruit juice and chunks of fresh pineapple for the grapefruit segments. Proceed as above and garnish as in the above recipe or with a pineapple core swizzle stick (page 37).

MANGO-SOY MILK SHAKE

Illustrated opposite.

A flavorful blend of mango and soy milk, with a hint of vanilla.

1 small or ½ large mango
1 cup soy milk, chilled (page 126)
Vanilla sugar (see note below)
Orange slice

1. Peel the mango and slice the flesh into a blender. If using a whole mango, squeeze the pit with your hands, making sure that all the juice is extracted from any flesh clinging to the pit.

2. Add the soy milk and blend until smooth. Add vanilla sugar to taste, then blend again.

3. Strain the blended mixture through a nylon sieve to remove any stringy bits of mango.

4. Pour into a tall glass and serve garnished with a slice of orange.

Note: To make Vanilla Sugar, place a whole vanilla bean in a covered jar of raw sugar and leave to stand for at least 2 weeks before using. The sugar will take on the flavor of the vanilla bean. Leave the vanilla bean in the jar of sugar, keeping it tightly covered, and use as required. Vanilla sugar is particularly good served with soy milk or coconut milk.

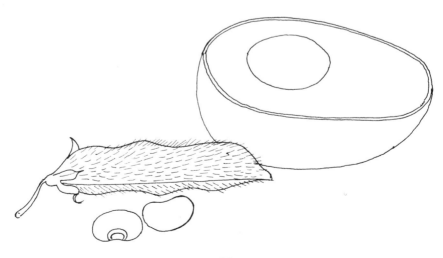

PALM BEACH

Apricot, orange juice, pineapple juice and cream are combined to make this flavorful cocktail.

1 large or 2 small apricots
6 tablespoons pineapple juice, chilled
6 tablespoons fresh orange juice, strained and chilled
2-3 tablespoons light cream
1 drop natural almond extract
Honey or raw cane sugar (optional)
Orange slices
Small paper parasol

1. Blanch the apricot(s) in boiling water for about 30 seconds, then plunge into cold water. (The skin should slip off easily.) Peel, cut in half and discard pit(s).

2. Slice the apricot flesh into a blender and add the pineapple and orange juices, cream and almond extract. Blend the ingredients until completely smooth. Taste and sweeten with a little honey or sugar, if necessary, then blend again.

3. Pour the mixture into a large cocktail glass and garnish with a few orange slices and a small, brightly-colored paper parasol.

Variation:
Prepare the drink in the same way, substituting fresh peach, nectarine or papaya for the apricot.

FROZEN PINEAPPLE AND BANANA DRINK

Pineapple juice and banana are blended with crushed ice to make this creamy, frozen drink.

²/₃ cup pineapple juice
1 small banana, peeled and chopped
1 cup crushed ice
Wedge of fresh pineapple

1. Place the pineapple juice, chopped banana and crushed ice in a blender. Blend together until creamy and slushy.

2. Pour, unstrained, into a drinks glass. Garnish with a wedge of fresh pineapple.

Variation:
Frozen Banana Milk Drink: Blend with ⅔ cup of milk and 1 cup of crushed ice. Pour, unstrained, into a drinks glass. Garnish with banana slices and cherries.

PAPAYA-STRAWBERRY COBBLER

This irresistible blend of exotic papaya and milk is served with fresh strawberries.

½ small papaya
1 cup milk, chilled
Honey or raw cane sugar (optional)
4 strawberries
Small flower

1. Peel and seed the papaya, then slice the flesh into a blender.
2. Add the milk and blend until completely smooth. Sweeten with a little honey or sugar, if necessary, then blend again.
3. Pour into a large glass.
4. Hull the strawberries, rinse in a colander and drain well. Slice the strawberries and add to the glass.
5. Garnish with a small flower and serve accompanied by an iced-tea spoon.

Variations:
Papaya-Nectarine Cobbler. Substitute peeled, diced nectarine for the strawberries. Proceed as above.
Papaya-Banana Cobbler. Following the same procedure as above, substitute sliced banana for the strawberries in the main recipe. (Diced apricot, peach or pineapple may also be added to this luscious drink.)

MELON MAGIC

Illustrated opposite.

This blend of succulent melon and pineapple juice is served in a melon shell.

1 small melon
²⁄₃ cup pineapple juice, chilled
Honey or raw cane sugar (optional)

1. Using a sharp knife, slice the top off the melon, reserving the lid and cutting a zig-zag pattern into the upper edge of the melon. Cut a thin slice off the bottom of the melon so that it will stand upright, taking care not to cut through the shell.

2. Scoop out the seeds from inside the melon and discard. Scoop out the flesh, leaving a thickness of about ½ inch around the sides and base of the shell so that it is quite sturdy.

3. Place the melon flesh in a blender, add the pineapple juice and blend until smooth. Taste and sweeten with a little honey or sugar, if you wish, then blend again.

4. Strain the mixture through a nylon sieve, then pour into the melon shell.

5. Pierce the reserved lid with a wooden toothpick and attach to the side of the melon, in the form of a slanted hat. Serve with straws.

Variation:
If preferred, substitute natural yogurt for the pineapple juice and proceed as above.

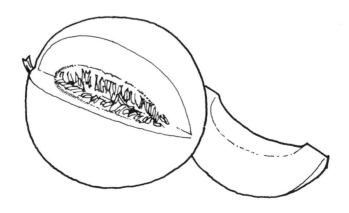

MIDSUMMER DREAM

Illustrated opposite.

A blend of apricot and orange juice is served with fresh strawberries and topped with a tangy layer of natural yogurt in this delectable summer fruit cocktail.

1 large or 2 small apricots
¾ cup fresh orange juice, strained and chilled
Honey or raw cane sugar (optional)
4 strawberries
1-2 tablespoons plain yogurt, chilled
2 tablespoons flaked almonds

1. Blanch the apricot(s) in boiling water for about 30 seconds, then plunge into cold water. (The skins should slip off easily.) Peel, cut fruit in half and discard pit(s).

2. Slice the apricot flesh into a blender, add the orange juice and blend until smooth. Taste and sweeten, if you wish, with a little honey or sugar, then blend again.

3. Pour into a tall, stemmed glass.

4. Hull and rinse the strawberries, draining well. Slice in half and add to the drink.

5. Lightly beat the yogurt with a spoon until smooth. Spoon over the top of the drink, allowing the yogurt to float, creating a contrasting layer of white against the orange and red. Garnish with flaked almonds. Serve accompanied by an iced-teaspoon.

Note: Try serving this delicious and nutritious cocktail as a light summer meal-in-a-glass.

PEACH AND OAT MILK COCKTAIL

A deliciously nutritious blend of juicy peach and flavorful oat milk.

1 peach
1 cup oat milk, chilled (page 125)
Finely grated orange zest
Orange slice
Small paper parasol

1. Blanch the peach in boiling water for about 30 seconds, then plunge into cold water. (The skin should slip off easily.) Peel, cut in half and discard pit.

2. Slice the peach flesh into a blender, add the oat milk and blend until completely smooth.

3. Pour into a tall glass and sprinkle with finely grated orange zest.

4. Garnish the drink with a slice of orange and a small, brightly-colored paper parasol.

Variations:
Apricot and Oat Milk Cocktail. Following the above procedure, substitute 1 large or 2 small apricots for the peach. Garnish as above.
Banana and Oat Milk Cocktail. Omit the peach and blend the oat milk with 1 small banana, sliced. Garnish as above.

PEACH MELBA COCKTAIL

An exquisite blend of peach, raspberries, milk and honey.

1 small peach
1/2 cup raspberries
1 cup milk, chilled
1-2 teaspoons clear honey
Raspberry or fresh herb leaves

1. Blanch the peach in boiling water for about 30 seconds, then plunge into cold water. (The skin should slip off easily.) Peel, cut in half and discard pit.

2. Slice the peach flesh into a blender.

3. Hull the raspberries, rinse in a colander and drain well. Reserve 2-3

raspberries for the garnish and place the remainder in the blender with the peach.

4. Add the milk and honey to the blender and blend until completely smooth.

5. Strain the mixture through a nylon sieve to remove the raspberry seeds and pour into a tall glass.

6. Garnish with the reserved raspberries and a sprig of raspberry or fresh herb leaves.

Variations:
Nectarine Melba Cocktail. Substitute 1 small nectarine for the peach and proceed as above.
Banana Melba Cocktail. Substitute 1 small banana for the peach. Add the raspberries, milk and honey and proceed as above.

PEAR-BUTTERMILK COCKTAIL

Ripe pear is blended with buttermilk, fresh lemon juice and honey in this creamy drink.

1 small, ripe pear
¾ cup buttermilk, chilled
2 teaspoons fresh lemon juice
1-2 teaspoons clear honey
Finely grated lemon zest
Twist of lemon peel

1. Peel and core the pear, then slice the flesh into a blender.

2. Add the buttermilk and lemon juice and blend until completely smooth.

3. Sweeten to taste with honey, then blend again.

4. Serve in a tall glass, topped with a sprinkling of finely grated lemon zest. Garnish with a twist of lemon peel.

Variation:
Banana Buttermilk Cocktail. Substitute 1 small banana, chopped, for the pear. Proceed as above.

MON CHERI

Illustrated opposite.

A deep red purée of raspberries and honey is combined with white grape juice to make this exquisite cocktail.

⅔ cup raspberries
1-2 teaspoons clear honey
6 tablespoons white grape juice, chilled
Small white flower

1. Hull the raspberries, rinse in a colander and drain well.

2. Press the raspberries through a nylon sieve to purée.

3. Add honey to the purée, sweetening to taste and blending well, so that the honey is thoroughly absorbed.

4. Strain the purée again, if necessary, ensuring that it is completely free of raspberry seeds.

5. Pour the raspberry-honey purée into a tall, stemmed glass and fill with grape juice. Stir and garnish with a small white flower.

Note: This cocktail makes an ideal party drink. Prepare the raspberry-honey purée in advance and keep chilled until required. When ready to serve, add the grape juice.

The proportion of grape juice and raspberry-honey purée can be varied to suit individual tastes. The greater amount of purée used, the more depth of color the drink will have.

Variation:
Mock Pink Champagne. Substitute sparkling white grape juice and proceed as above.

PARADISE

Nectarine, strawberries and pineapple juice are combined to make this luscious cocktail.

1 small nectarine
6 strawberries
¾ cup pineapple juice, chilled
Honey or raw cane sugar (optional)
Strawberry or fresh herb leaves

1. Blanch the nectarine in boiling water for about 30 seconds, then plunge into cold water. (The skin should slip off easily.) Peel, cut fruit in half and discard pit.

2. Slice the nectarine flesh into a blender.

3. Hull and rinse the strawberries, draining well. Reserve 2 strawberries for garnish and place the remainder in the blender.

4. Add the pineapple juice and blend until completely smooth. Taste and sweeten, if necessary, with a little honey or sugar, then blend again.

5. Strain the mixture and pour into a large cocktail glass, garnishing with the reserved strawberries and a sprig of strawberry or fresh herb leaves.

Variation:
Prepare the cocktail with 1 small peach or apricot, instead of the nectarine, if preferred.

GRAPE AND PINEAPPLE PUNCH

A delicious punch made with grape juice, pineapple juice, lemon juice and honey, served with grapes and chunks of fresh pineapple.

½ cup white grape juice, chilled
½ cup pineapple juice, chilled
Juice of ½ lemon, strained
1 teaspoon clear honey
Green grapes, seeded
Chunks of fresh pineapple
Twist of lemon peel

1. Mix the grape, pineapple and lemon juices together. Pour into a tall glass and add the honey, stirring well so that the honey is thoroughly absorbed.

2. Add some green grapes and chunks of fresh pineapple to the mixed juices. Garnish with a bright twist of lemon peel. Serve the punch accompanied by an iced-tea spoon.

Note: If you prefer a sharper-flavored punch, prepare the mixed juices without adding honey. Substitute lime juice for lemon juice.

PASSION FRUIT-PEACH MILK SHAKE

Fresh peach is blended with passion fruit-flavored milk in this delicately fragrant milk shake.

1 passion fruit
1 cup milk, chilled
1 peach
Honey or raw cane sugar (optional)
Twist of orange peel

1. Cut the passion fruit in half and scoop out the seedy pulp with a spoon.

2. Place the passion fruit pulp in a nylon sieve. Strain the milk through the sieve, over the pulp, pressing the passion fruit seeds with the back of a spoon, making sure that the fruit juice and pulp are separated from the seeds. Repeat the straining process several times to ensure that the full flavor of the passion fruit is contained in the milk, with only bare black seeds remaining in the sieve. Discard the seeds.

3. Blanch the peach in boiling water for about 30 seconds, then plunge into cold water. (The skin should slip off easily.) Peel, cut the peach in half and discard pit.

4. Slice the peach flesh into a blender and add the passion fruit-flavored milk. Blend until completely smooth. Taste and add a little honey or sugar if you wish to sweeten, then blend again. (Take care not to over-sweeten as this will destroy the delicate flavor of the passion fruit.)

5. Serve in a tall glass, garnished with a twist of orange peel.

Variation:
Passion Fruit-Pineapple Milk Shake. Omit the peach. Substitute 3 tablespoons chopped pineapple, adding to the blender with the passion fruit-flavored milk. Blend until smooth, strain into a tall glass and garnish with a wedge of fresh pineapple.

MONT BLANC

Illustrated opposite.

A blend of red grape juice and natural yogurt, reminiscent of a snow-capped peak.

½ cup red grape juice, chilled
6 tablespoons plain yogurt, chilled
Black grapes or black cherries
1 teaspoon plain yogurt

1. Mix the grape juice and yogurt, blending thoroughly.

2. Pour into a cocktail glass and garnish with black grapes or black cherries.

3. Just before serving, spoon the yogurt over the top, allowing it to float, creating the effect of a snow-capped mountain.

Note: As red grape juice is naturally sweet, you should not need to add additional sugar or honey to this cocktail.

MONTMARTRE

A delicious blend of flavors is contained in this drink made with pear, banana, natural yogurt and honey.

1 small or ½ large pear
½ banana
¾ cup plain yogurt, chilled
1-2 teaspoons clear honey
Finely grated orange zest
Twist of orange peel
Small flower

1. Peel and core the pear, then slice the flesh into a blender.

2. Peel and slice the banana into the blender and add yogurt and honey to taste. Blend all the ingredients until completely smooth.

3. Pour the mixture into a tall glass and sprinkle with finely grated orange zest. To add color to the drink, garnish with a twist of orange peel and a small, brightly-colored flower.

PERSIMMON-ORANGE YOGURT DRINK

Persimmon is blended with orange juice and natural yogurt in this creamy drink.

1 ripe persimmon
6 tablespoons fresh orange juice, strained and chilled
6 tablespoons plain yogurt, chilled
Honey or raw cane sugar (optional)
Orange slice
Finely grated orange zest

1. Peel the persimmon and slice the flesh into a blender.

2. Add the orange juice and yogurt and blend until smooth. Taste and sweeten with a little honey or sugar, if necessary, then blend again.

3. Pour into a large cocktail glass and garnish with an orange slice and finely grated orange zest.

Variations:
Persimmon-Pineapple Yogurt Drink. Substitute pineapple juice for the orange juice. Proceed as above and garnish with a wedge of fresh pineapple.
Persimmon-Mandarin Yogurt Drink. Substitute fresh mandarin orange juice for the regular orange juice. Proceed as above, garnishing with mandarin orange segments and finely grated mandarin orange peel.
Persimmon-Mandarin Drink. Omit the yogurt. Add ¾ cup fresh mandarin orange juice to the persimmon in the blender and proceed as above, garnishing with mandarin orange segments and finely grated mandarin orange peel.

PINEAPPLE ALASKA

Pineapple juice, crushed ice, egg white and maple syrup are combined to make this eye-catching cooler.

¾ cup pineapple juice
1 cup crushed ice
½ egg white
1-2 teaspoons pure maple syrup
Wedge of fresh pineapple

1. Place the pineapple juice, crushed ice and egg white into a blender. Blend until smooth and creamy.

2. Pour unstrained into a large, shallow cocktail glass. Set the glass aside for a minute or two. The egg white will rise to the top, leaving the pineapple juice and crushed ice in the base.

3. After the egg white head rises, drizzle the maple syrup over it. Garnish with a wedge of fresh pineapple.

PINEAPPLE-CUCUMBER DRINK

The delicate flesh of the cucumber is blended with pineapple juice in this refreshing beverage.

2-inch piece of cucumber
¾ cup pineapple juice, chilled
Spiral of cucumber peel

1. Peel the cucumber, cutting the peel away from the flesh in a long spiral. Reserve.

2. Slice the peeled cucumber flesh into a blender, add the pineapple juice and blend until smooth.

3. Strain the mixture and serve in a cocktail glass, garnished with the spiral of cucumber peel.

Variation:
Pineapple-Cucumber Cobbler. Blend the pineapple juice and cucumber flesh, as above. Strain into a tall glass and add chunks of fresh pineapple and cubes of cucumber, garnishing with a spiral of cucumber peel and accompanying the drink with an iced-tea spoon.

MOONLIGHT

Illustrated opposite.

White grape juice, egg white and pure maple syrup are combined to make this light and bright drink.

¾ cup white grape juice, chilled
½ egg white
1-2 teaspoons pure maple syrup

1. Blend the grape juice with the egg white at high speed until creamy and frothy.

2. Pour into a large cocktail glass and set aside for several minutes, allowing the egg white to separate from the juice.

3. Drizzle the maple syrup over the egg white and serve accompanied by an iced-tea spoon.

PEARL OF THE ORIENT

An Eastern delight of mandarin orange juice, pineapple juice and lychees.

½ cup fresh mandarin orange juice
¼ cup pineapple juice
Crushed ice
4-6 lychee nuts, peeled and stoned

1. Combine the mandarin orange and pineapple juices.

2. Half-fill a shallow Champagne glass with crushed ice and place the lychees on top of the ice.

3. Strain the mixed juices over the lychees and ice and serve immediately, accompanied by an iced-tea spoon.

PEAR-PINEAPPLE COCKTAIL

This simple combination of ripe pear and pineapple juice is refreshingly sweet and fruity.

1 small, ripe pear
¾ cup pineapple juice, chilled
Seedless green grapes or slice of kiwi fruit

1. Peel and core the pear, then slice the flesh into a blender.

2. Add the pineapple juice and blend until completely smooth.

3. Serve the cocktail in a tall glass, garnished with a small cluster of green grapes or a slice of kiwi fruit.

Variation:
Pear-Mandarin Cocktail. Substitute fresh mandarin orange juice for the pineapple juice. Garnish with mandarin orange segments.

PERFECT LOVE

A perfectly luscious blend of exotic papaya, fragrant passion fruit and pineapple juice.

1 passion fruit
¾ cup pineapple juice, chilled
½ small papaya
Small flowers

1. Cut the passion fruit in half and scoop out the seedy pulp with a spoon.

2. Place the passion fruit pulp in a nylon sieve. Strain the pineapple juice through the sieve, over the pulp, pressing the passion fruit seeds with the back of a spoon, making sure that the fruit juice and pulp are separated from the seeds. Repeat the straining process several times to ensure that the full flavor of the passion fruit is contained in the pineapple juice, with only bare black seeds remaining in the sieve. Discard the seeds.

3. Peel and seed the papaya. Use a melon baller to make 2 papaya balls and reserve them for the garnish.

4. Slice the remaining papaya flesh into a blender and add the passion fruit-flavored pineapple juice. Blend until completely smooth.

5. Serve in a tall glass, garnished with the reserved papaya balls and a few small, brightly-colored flowers.

ORANGE AND PASSION FRUIT FRAPPE

Illustrated opposite.

Fresh orange juice is flavored with the delicately fragrant and delicious juice of the passion fruit in this tempting frappé.

1 passion fruit
¾ cup fresh orange juice
Crushed ice
Orange slices
Cherries

1. Cut the passion fruit in half and scoop out the seedy pulp with a spoon.

2. Place the passion fruit pulp in a nylon sieve, then strain the orange juice through the sieve, over the pulp, pressing the passion fruit seeds with the back of a spoon, making sure that the fruit juice and pulp are separated from the seeds. Repeat the straining process several times to ensure that the full flavor of the passion fruit is contained in the orange juice, with only bare black seeds remaining in the sieve. Discard the seeds.

3. Fill a large cocktail glass with crushed ice, then pour the orange-passion fruit juice over the ice.

4. Garnish with orange slices and cherries.

Variation:
Pineapple-Passion Fruit Frappé. Substitute pineapple juice for the orange juice, following the same procedure as above. Garnish with a wedge of fresh pineapple.

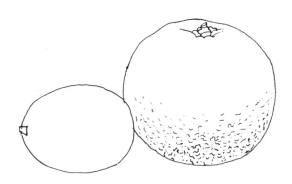

RASPBERRY-PINEAPPLE COCKTAIL

Rich red raspberries are blended with pineapple juice in this refreshingly fruity cocktail.

2/3 cup raspberries
3/4 cup pineapple juice, chilled
Honey or raw cane sugar (optional)
Raspberry or fresh herb leaves

1. Hull the raspberries, rinse in a colander and drain well. Reserve 2-3 raspberries for the garnish.

2. Place the remainder of the raspberries in a blender, add the pineapple juice and blend until smooth. Taste and sweeten with a little honey or sugar if you wish, then blend again.

3. Strain the mixture to remove the raspberry seeds.

4. Pour into a tall, stemmed glass and garnish with the reserved raspberries and a contrasting sprig of raspberry or fresh herb leaves.

Variation:
Raspberry-Orange Cocktail. Substitute orange juice for the pineapple juice, and a twist of orange peel for the raspberry or herb leaves. Proceed as above.

RASPBERRY RIPPLE

A flavorsome blend of fresh raspberries, natural yogurt, milk and honey, rippled with raspberry purée.

1 scant cup raspberries
1/2 cup plain yogurt, chilled
1/4 cup milk, chilled
1-2 teaspoons clear honey
Raspberry or fresh herb leaves

1. Hull the raspberries, rinse in a colander and drain well. Reserve 2-3 raspberries for the garnish.

2. Place 2/3 cup raspberries in a blender with the yogurt, milk and honey. Blend until smooth.

3. Strain the mixture into a large cocktail glass.

4. Press the remaining raspberries through a nylon sieve, to purée.

5.   Drizzle the raspberry purée over the drink, creating a ripple effect. Garnish with the reserved raspberries and a sprig of raspberry or fresh herb leaves.

Variations:
Strawberry Ripple. Substitute strawberries for the raspberries and follow the above procedure.
Black Currant Ripple. Substitute fresh black currants for the raspberries and proceed as above.

ROSE OF PICARDY

Illustrated on page 77.

Rich, fruity red grape juice is blended with egg white to create this colorful crimson-pink cocktail.

³/₄ cup red grape juice
¹/₂ egg white
Small white or pink flower

1.   Blend the grape juice and egg white at high speed until creamy and frothy. Pour into a tall glass and set aside for several minutes to allow the foamy egg white to separate from the juice.

2.   When ready to serve, garnish with a small white or pink flower.

Note: This drink has two colorfully contrasting layers — a deep crimson base, topped with a delicate pink head.

ORANGE AND CARROT COCKTAIL

Fresh orange juice is blended with grated raw carrot in this flavorful fruit and vegetable cocktail.

1 carrot
3/4 cup fresh orange juice, chilled
Carrot sticks (see note below)
Sprig of watercress or parsley

1. Scrape the carrot and grate into a blender.

2. Add the orange juice and blend until smooth.

3. Strain mixture into a tall glass and garnish with carrot sticks and a sprig of watercress or parsley.

Note: To make carrot sticks, pare a long, thin carrot with a vegetable peeler and cut lengthwise into 4 strips. Cut into stick shapes and use as swizzle sticks to garnish vegetable juice cocktails.

ORANGE YOGURT CUP

Illustrated opposite.

This blend of fresh orange and yogurt is served in an orange shell.

1 navel orange
2/3 cup plain yogurt, chilled
Honey or raw cane sugar (optional)

1. Using a sharp knife, slice the top off the orange. Scoop the flesh from the top and reserve the lid. Cut a zig-zag pattern along the top edge of the orange. Scoop out the flesh, taking care not to puncture the shell.

2. Place the orange flesh and yogurt in a blender and blend until smooth. Taste and sweeten with a little honey or sugar, if necessary, then blend again.

3. Strain the orange-yogurt mixture through a nylon sieve, then pour into the reserved orange shell. Pierce the lid with a toothpick and attach to the side of the orange shell, in the form of a slanted hat. Serve with straws.

SIERRA NEVADA

This blend of pineapple juice and orange juice is capped with a lovely, snowy egg white froth.

6 tablespoons pineapple juice, chilled
6 tablespoons fresh orange juice, chilled
1/2 egg white

1. Combine the juices, then strain into a blender.
2. Add the egg white and blend at high speed for about 30 seconds, so that the egg white is thoroughly blended.
3. Pour the mixture into a tall tumbler and set aside for a few minutes. The frothy egg white will separate from the juice and rise to the top, creating a lovely, snowy head.

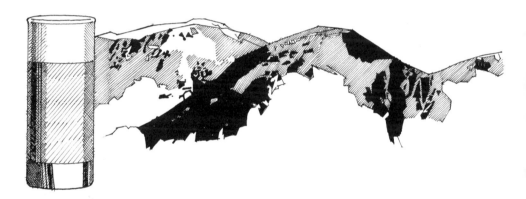

SORRENTO COOLER

A long, cool drink consisting of luscious peach, fresh orange juice, lime juice and sparkling mineral water.

1 peach
1/2 cup fresh orange juice, strained and chilled
Juice of 1/2 lime, strained
Sparkling mineral water or club soda, chilled
Honey or raw cane sugar (optional)
Slice of orange
Twist of lime peel

1. Blanch the peach in boiling water for about 30 seconds, then plunge into cold water. (The skin should slip off easily.) Peel, cut in half and discard pit.

2. Slice the peach flesh into a blender, add orange and lime juices and blend until completely smooth.

3. Pour the mixture into a tall glass and fill with mineral or soda water, stirring well. Taste and add a little honey or sugar to sweeten, if necessary, and stir again thoroughly to combine.

4. Garnish with a slice of orange and a twist of lime peel.

Variation:
Following the same procedure, prepare the drink with fresh apricot or nectarine instead of peach.

SOUTH SEAS COCKTAIL

A sunshine blend of banana, pineapple juice and lime juice.

1 small or ½ large banana, peeled and sliced
¾ cup pineapple juice, chilled
Juice of ½ lime, strained
Finely grated lime zest
Twist of lime peel
Small flowers

1. Place the banana, pineapple and lime juices in a blender and blend until smooth and creamy.

2. Pour the liquid into a tall glass and top with a sprinkling of finely grated lime zest.

3. To serve, garnish with a twist of lime peel and a few small, brightly-colored flowers.

87

PINEAPPLE-CHERRY COBBLER

Illustrated opposite.

A refreshing drink made with pineapple juice and lime juice, served with chunks of fresh pineapple and fresh cherries.

Juice of 1 lime
1 cup pineapple juice, chilled
2 slices fresh pineapple
4-6 fresh cherries, pitted

1. Strain the lime juice into a large glass, then add the pineapple juice, stirring well.

2. Cut the pineapple into chunks and add to the mixed juices along with the cherries. Serve accompanied by an iced-tea spoon.

Variations:
Pineapple-Mango Cobbler. Substitute diced mango for the cherries. Proceed as above.
Pineapple-Peach Cobbler. Following the above procedure, substitute diced peach for the cherries. (Nectarines or apricots are also delicious served in this way.)

STRAWBERRY MILK FRAPPE

This delicious blend of fresh strawberries, milk and honey is poured over crushed ice.

8 strawberries
¾ cup milk
1-2 teaspoons clear honey
Crushed ice
Strawberry or fresh herb leaves

1. Hull the strawberries, rinse in a colander and drain well. Reserve 2 strawberries for the garnish.

2. Place the remainder of the strawberries in a blender with the milk and honey and blend until completely smooth.

3. Strain the mixture to remove the strawberry seeds.

4. Fill a large cocktail glass with crushed ice. Pour the strawberry milk over the ice and garnish with the reserved strawberries and a few strawberry or fresh herb leaves.

Variation:
Strawberry Cream Frappé. Reduce the milk in the above recipe to ⅔ cup. Add 2 tablespoons light cream and blend as above.

STRAWBERRY-ORANGE COCKTAIL

A taste of summer sun is contained in this blend of fresh strawberries and orange juice.

6 strawberries
¾ cup fresh orange juice, chilled
Honey or raw cane sugar (optional)
Twist of orange peel
Small paper parasol

1. Hull the strawberries, rinse in a colander and drain well. Reserve 1 strawberry for the garnish.

2. Place the remaining strawberries in a blender. Add the orange juice and blend until completely smooth. Taste and add a little honey or sugar to sweeten, if you wish, then blend again.

3. Strain mixture to remove the strawberry seeds.

4. Pour mixture into a large cocktail glass and garnish with the reserved strawberry, a twist of orange peel and a small paper parasol.

Variations:
Strawberry-Orange Frappé. Prepare the drink as above and, after straining, pour the mixture into a glass packed with crushed ice. Garnish as above.
Strawberry-Pineapple Cocktail. Prepare as above, substituting pineapple juice for the orange juice. Add a sprig of strawberry or fresh herb leaves to the garnish. (This combination is also delicious served as a frappé cocktail, poured over a mountain of crushed ice.)

STRAWBERRY PUNCH

A delectable fruity punch made of strawberries, pineapple juice and grape juice, laden with fresh fruit.

8 strawberries
2/3 cup pineapple juice, chilled
6 tablespoons white grape juice, chilled
Chunks of fresh pineapple
Seedless green grapes
Small paper parasol

1. Hull the strawberries, rinse in a colander and drain well. Reserve 2 strawberries for the garnish.

2. Place the remaining strawberries in a blender, add the pineapple and grape juices and blend until completely smooth.

3. Strain the mixture to remove the strawberry seeds and pour into a large glass.

4. Slice the remaining strawberries and add to the punch, together with a few chunks of pineapple and some grapes.

5. Garnish with a small, brightly-colored paper parasol and serve accompanied by an iced-tea spoon.

PINEAPPLE-COCONUT COCKTAIL

Illustrated opposite.

A non-alcoholic version of the Piña Colada, made with coconut milk, fresh pineapple and lime juice.

¾ cup coconut milk, chilled (page 124)
4 tablespoons chopped pineapple
1 teaspoon fresh lime juice
Honey or raw cane sugar (optional)
Cherries or wedge of fresh pineapple

1. Place the coconut milk, pineapple and lime juice in a blender and blend until smooth. Add a little honey or sugar to taste, if you wish, then blend again.

2. Strain mixture through a nylon sieve and pour into a tall, stemmed glass.

3. Garnish with cherries or a wedge of fresh pineapple.

Variation:
Mango-Coconut Cocktail. Substitute the flesh of ½ mango for the chopped pineapple and proceed as above, garnishing the cocktail with cherries and/or chunks of diced mango.

VANILLA-PEACH MILK SHAKE

A deliciously tempting blend of vanilla-flavored milk and fresh peach.

1 peach
1 cup vanilla milk, chilled (page 126)
Cherries
Twist of orange peel

1. Blanch the peach in boiling water for about 30 seconds, then plunge into cold water. (The skin should slip off easily.) Peel, cut in half and discard pit.

2. Slice the peach flesh into a blender, add the vanilla milk and blend until completely smooth.

3. Pour into a tall glass and garnish with a few cherries and a twist of orange peel.

Variation:
Vanilla Banana Milk Shake. Substitute 1 peeled and sliced banana with for the peach. Garnish as above. (Apricot, nectarine, papaya and pear are also delicious blended with vanilla milk.)

VIE-EN-ROSE

This deep-pink, delectable drink is a blend of red grape juice, raspberries, natural yogurt and honey.

1/2 cup raspberries
3/4 cup red grape juice, chilled
1-2 teaspoons clear honey
1 tablespoon plain yogurt
Small white or pink flowers

1. Hull the raspberries, rinse in a colander and drain well.

2. Place the raspberries in a blender with the grape juice and honey, blending until completely smooth.

3. Strain the mixture to remove the raspberry seeds.

4. Reserve 1 teaspoon of the mixture, spoon the yogurt into the blender container and blend thoroughly.

5. Pour the liquid into a tall glass.

6. Just before serving, drizzle the reserved raspberry-grape juice over the drink. The red juice makes an attractive contrast to the deep-pink liquid. A garnish of small white or pink flowers is ideal for this colourful drink.

WAIKIKI KISS

The flesh of a fresh pineapple is combined with orange juice and served in the pineapple shell in this temptingly exotic blend.

1 small, ripe pineapple
½-⅔ cup fresh orange juice, chilled
Honey or raw cane sugar (optional)

1. Slice the top off the pineapple, reserving the tuft of leaves for the garnish.

2. Slice a little off the bottom of the pineapple, so that it will stand upright, taking care not to puncture the flesh.

3. Using a sharp knife, extract the pineapple flesh, leaving the shell base and sides approximately ½-inch thick, to provide a sturdy container for the drink.

4. Place the pineapple flesh in a blender and blend to a smooth purée, adding enough orange juice to produce a drinkable consistency. Taste and sweeten, if necessary, with a little honey or sugar. Blend again.

5. Strain and pour the liquid into the prepared pineapple shell.

6. Trim the tuft of pineapple leaves, discarding any withered parts. Place straws in the pineapple shell and garnish with the pineapple leaves.

Variation:
The pineapple flesh may be blended with chilled milk, natural yogurt or white grape juice, instead of orange juice, using the above procedure.

PINK HEAVEN

Illustrated opposite.

Fresh strawberries, natural yogurt, milk and honey are blended together in this heavenly cocktail.

4-6 strawberries
½ cup plain yogurt, chilled
¼ cup milk, chilled
1-2 teaspoons clear honey

1. Hull the strawberries, rinse in a colander and drain well.

2. Place the strawberries in a blender and add the yogurt, milk and honey. Blend until completely smooth.

3. Strain to remove the strawberry seeds, pour into a cocktail glass and serve.

Variation:
Prepare by the above method, substituting raspberries for strawberries.

PINEAPPLE-PEACH YOGURT DRINK

A deliciously nutritious blend of fresh peach, pineapple juice and natural yogurt.

1 peach
6 tablespoons pineapple juice, chilled
6 tablespoons plain yogurt, chilled
Honey or raw cane sugar (optional)

1. Blanch the peach in boiling water for about 30 seconds, then plunge into cold water. (The skin should slip off easily.) Peel, cut in half and discard pit. Reserve a slice of peach for garnish.

2. Slice the remaining peach flesh into a blender and add the pineapple juice and yogurt. Blend until completely smooth. If you wish to sweeten, add a little honey or sugar to taste, then blend again.

3. Pour into a cocktail glass, dice the reserved peach slice and place on top of the drink as garnish.

Variation:
Following the same procedure, prepare the cocktail with apricot, nectarine, mango or papaya instead of peach.

ST. LUCIA PUNCH

Illustrated on page 100.

Transport yourself to a land of azure blue skies and swaying palm trees with this lusciously long and refreshing drink of fresh lime juice, pineapple juice and orange juice, served with fresh fruit and exotically garnished with flowers.

Juice of 1 lime
½ cup pineapple juice, chilled
½ cup fresh orange juice, chilled
1 slice fresh pineapple
2 slices cucumber, pared
Seedless green grapes
Cantaloupe melon balls
Small flowers

1. Combine the lime, pineapple and orange juices, then strain into a tall glass.

2. Cut half the slice of pineapple into chunks. Dice 1 slice of cucumber and add these to the drink, along with a few grapes and melon balls.

3. Cut the remaining pineapple into 2 wedges and fix onto the side of the glass. Spear the remaining slice of cucumber, some additional grapes and melon balls on a toothpick and attach to one of the pineapple wedges. Complete the garnish by adding a few small, colorful flowers. Serve accompanied by an iced-tea spoon.

Variation:
Using the three mixed juices as a base, prepare the punch with any of your favorite seasonal fruits, making the drink look as colorful and refreshing as possible.

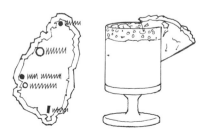

TROPICAL NECTAR

Illustrated on page 101.

A taste of the tropics is contained in this cocktail made from passion fruit, papaya, banana, nectarine and pineapple juice.

1 passion fruit
1 cup pineapple juice, chilled
1 tablespoon each peeled, diced papaya, banana and nectarine
Pineapple core swizzle stick (page 37)

1. Cut the passion fruit in half and scoop out the seedy pulp with a spoon.

2. Place the passion fruit pulp in a nylon sieve. Strain the pineapple juice through the sieve, over the pulp, pressing the passion fruit seeds with the back of a spoon, making sure that the fruit juice and pulp are separated from the seeds. Repeat the straining process several times to ensure that the full flavor of the passion fruit is contained in the pineapple juice, with only bare black seeds remaining in the sieve. Discard the seeds.

3. Place the passion fruit-flavored pineapple juice in a blender and add the papaya, banana and nectarine. Blend until completely smooth.

4. Pour the mixture into a tall glass and serve, exotically garnished with a pineapple core swizzle stick.

Variations:
Tropical Nectar may be prepared with any of your favorite exotic fruits. Use the pineapple-passion fruit juice as the base, blending it with any combination of exotic fruits that you fancy. You will need approximately 3 tablespoons of combined fruits.

QUARTIER LATIN

Illustrated on page 11.

Apricot, banana and fresh orange juice are combined to make this flavor-rich drink.

1 small apricot
½ banana, peeled and sliced
¾ cup fresh orange juice, strained and chilled
Orange slice
Small flower

1. Blanch the apricot in boiling water for about 30 seconds, then plunge into cold water. (The skin should slip off easily.) Peel, cut in half and discard pit.

2. Slice the apricot flesh into a blender, add the banana and orange juice and blend until completely smooth and creamy.

3. Pour into a large cocktail glass and garnish with a slice of orange and a small, brightly-colored flower.

Variation:
Prepare the drink with pineapple juice instead of orange juice, or a combination of orange and pineapple juices, following the above method.

WEDDING BELLE

Illustrated opposite.

This blend of orange juice, pineapple juice, nectarine and honey is veiled with egg white and garnished with a delicate little flower.

6 tablespoons fresh orange juice, strained and chilled
6 tablespoons pineapple juice, chilled
1 nectarine
1 teaspoon clear honey
½ egg white
Small yellow or white flower

1. Pour the orange and pineapple juices into a blender.

2. Blanch the nectarine in boiling water for about 30 seconds, then plunge into cold water. (The skin should slip off easily.) Peel, cut in half and discard pit.

3. Slice the nectarine flesh into the blender, add the honey and blend until smooth.

4. Pour the mixture into a tall glass (a Champagne flute is ideal).

5. Whisk the egg white until it stands in soft peaks, then spoon enough over the cocktail so that it is veiled in white. Garnish with a small yellow or white flower.

Variation:
Prepare the drink with peach or apricot instead of nectarine, if preferred.

WATERMELON-PINEAPPLE PUNCH

The juicy flesh of the watermelon is blended with pineapple juice and served with chunks of fresh pineapple in this refreshing punch.

3 tablespoons chopped watermelon flesh, seeded
3/4 cup pineapple juice, chilled
Chunks of fresh pineapple
Wedge of watermelon
Small paper parasol

1. Place the watermelon flesh and pineapple juice in a blender and blend until completely smooth.

2. Pour mixture into a tall glass and add chunks of fresh pineapple.

3. Garnish with a wedge of watermelon and a small paper parasol. Serve accompanied with an iced-tea spoon.

Variation:
Watermelon-Orange Punch. Substitute orange juice for the pineapple juice. Replace the chunks of fresh pineapple with orange segments and garnish as above.

2.
DRIED FRUIT DRINKS

Dried fruits have the advantage of being readily available all year round. They are immensely rich in flavor and packed with essential vitamins and minerals. Moreover, with their high concentration of natural sugars, they rarely require additional sweetening when used in drinks.

To soften dried fruits that will be blended into drinks, it is necessary to soak them overnight in liquid — preferably fruit juice or milk. The flavor of dried fruit drinks can be enhanced by adding a strip of lemon or orange peel, a small cinnamon stick, or a piece of vanilla bean to the soaking liquid. Lemon peel is particularly good as a flavor enhancer in dried pear and apple drinks, whereas dried apricot and peach drinks are made more appealing by adding a strip of orange peel, or a split, unblanched almond to the soaking liquid. Cinnamon and vanilla are good flavorants in milk-based drinks.

It is essential to use soft, plump dried fruits, not those that are excessively dry or wrinkled. If the fruit is over-dry (a sign of age), it will fail to soften fully during the soaking period and will be more difficult to blend. It is also worth remembering to cover the dried fruits and liquid with plastic wrap during the soaking period so that the concentrated aroma of the fruit is retained. This will also prevent any extraneous odors that may be in your refrigerator from penetrating the soaking liquid.

There are almost as many possible drinks combinations for dried fruit as there are for those made with fresh fruits, and once again, creativity and experimentation are the keys to success. Because of the good keeping qualities of dried fruits, the makings for the most delicious, nutritious and stunningly attractive fruit drinks can be kept readily available on your kitchen shelves.

ALHAMBRA

This delicately fragrant, delectable blend of dried peach and apricots, passion fruit juice, pineapple juice and orange juice is topped with a contrasting white, wispy layer of egg white.

½ cup pineapple juice
½ cup fresh orange juice
½ passion fruit
1 dried peach
2 dried apricots
½ egg white

1. Combine the pineapple and orange juices.

2. Scoop out the seedy pulp from the passion fruit and add it to the mixed juices.

3. Soak the dried peach and apricots in the mixed juices overnight.

4. Strain the juices into a blender, adding the soaked, dried fruit to the sieve.

5. Press the passion fruit seeds remaining in the sieve with the back of a spoon, so that all the fragrant juice is separated from the seeds. Discard the seeds.

6. Blend the dried fruits and juices until completely smooth.

7. Strain the mixture, then pour into a tall glass.

8. Whisk the egg white until it stands in soft peaks, then spoon over the liquid, allowing it to float on top and create a wispy, white contrast to the golden base.

9. Garnish with a small yellow or white flower.

APPLE-FIG MILK SHAKE

Dried apple rings and dried fig are soaked in milk with a strip of lemon peel to make this delicious and nutritious milk shake.

1 dried fig
4 medium, dried apple rings
Thinly pared strip of lemon peel
1 cup milk
Finely grated lemon zest
Twist of lemon peel

1. Soak the dried fig, apple rings and strip of lemon peel in the milk overnight.
2. Discard the lemon peel, pour fruits and milk into a blender and blend until completely smooth.
3. Strain the mixture into a tall glass. Sprinkle with finely grated lemon zest.
4. Add a bright twist of lemon peel to garnish.

Variation:
Pear-Fig Milk Shake. Substitute 1 dried pear half for the apple rings in the above recipe, following the same procedure.

APPLE-GRAPE DRINK

The sweet flavors of apples and grapes are perfectly matched in this ambrosial cocktail.

6 medium dried apple rings
1 cup white grape juice
Small cluster of seedless green grapes

1. Soak the dried apple rings in the grape juice overnight.
2. Place the apple rings and grape juice in a blender and blend until completely smooth.
3. Serve in a tall glass, garnished with a small cluster of grapes.

Variation:

Apple-Grape Yogurt Drink. Follow the above procedure. After blending float 1 tablespoon natural yogurt on top of the drink and garnish as above.

APPLE-SULTANA MILK SHAKE

A hint of cinnamon enhances the flavor of this blend of dried apples, golden raisins and milk.

4 dried apple rings
Small handful of golden seedless raisins (10-12)
1 inch cinnamon stick
1 cup milk
Twist of orange peel

1. Soak the dried apple rings, raisins and cinnamon stick in the milk overnight.

2. Remove the cinnamon stick, and pour the mixture into a blender. Blend until completely smooth.

3. Strain and serve the drink in a tall glass. Garnish with a bright twist of orange peel to add some color.

Variation:

Apple-Raisin Milk Shake. Substitute dark raisins for the golden seedless variety and proceed as above.

APRICOT-ORANGE YOGURT COCKTAIL

A sweet blend of dried apricots and orange juice is combined with natural yogurt in this flavorful drink.

2 medium or 3 small dried apricots
1 cup fresh orange juice
1 tablespoon plain yogurt
Finely grated orange zest
Twist of orange peel

1. Soak the dried apricots overnight in the orange juice.

2. Place the apricots and orange juice in a blender and blend until completely smooth.

3. Add the yogurt and blend again. Strain and pour the liquid into a tall glass.

4. Sprinkle with finely grated orange zest and garnish with a twist of orange peel.

Variation:
Apricot-Pineapple Yogurt Cocktail. Substitute pineapple juice for the orange juice and proceed as above.

EASTERN PROMISE

The exotic flavors of mandarin orange juice and apricots are contained in this luscious, deeply-colored drink.

3 medium or 4 small dried apricots
Thinly pared strip of mandarin orange peel
1 cup fresh mandarin orange juice
Small flower

1. Soak the dried apricots and mandarin orange peel in the mandarin orange juice overnight.

2. Discard the orange peel. Place the soaked fruit and juice in a blender and blend until smooth.

3. Strain and pour the liquid into a tall glass.

4. Garnish with a small, exotic-looking flower.

Variation:
Substitute dried peaches for the apricots and proceed as above.

MONTSERRAT

A sweet, creamy blend of dried apricots and milk, with a hint of almond flavor.

3 medium or 4 small dried apricots
1 cup milk
2 unblanched, whole almonds
Finely grated orange zest
Twist of orange peel
Small flower

1. Place the dried apricots in the milk. Split the almonds lengthwise, add to the apricot-milk mixture and soak overnight. (This will add a delicate almond flavor.)

2. Remove the almonds, place the apricots and milk in a blender and blend until smooth and creamy.

3. Strain the mixture and pour into a tall glass.

4. Top with a sprinkling of finely grated orange zest to add some color to the drink and garnish with a twist of orange peel and a small, brightly-colored flower.

PARIS BY NIGHT

Dried pear, passion fruit juice and milk are combined to make this sweet, delicately fragrant cocktail.

2 dried pear halves
Thinly pared strip of orange peel
1 cup milk
½ passion fruit
Orange slice
Small flower

1. Place the dried pear halves and strip of orange peel in the milk.

2. Scoop out the seedy pulp from the passion fruit, add to the pear-milk mixture and soak overnight.

3. Strain the milk into a blender and add the soaked pear halves. Press the passion fruit seeds remaining in the sieve with the back of a spoon, so that all the fragrant juice is separated from the seeds. Discard the seeds and orange peel.

4. Blend the mixture until completely smooth.

5. Strain and serve in a tall glass, garnished with an orange slice and a small, brightly-colored flower.

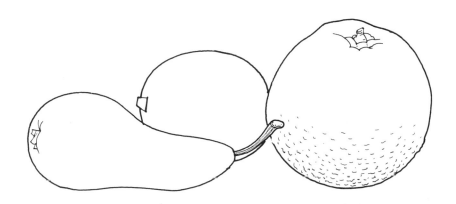

PEACH-PINEAPPLE COCKTAIL

This golden liquid is full of the aroma and flavor of sun-kissed peaches.

2 medium or 3 small dried peaches
1 cup pineapple juice
Twist of orange peel
Small paper parasol

1. Soak the dried peaches overnight in the pineapple juice.

2. Place the fruit and juice in a blender and blend until completely smooth.

3. Strain the mixture and serve in a tall glass, garnished with a twist of orange peel and a small, brightly-colored paper parasol.

Variation:
Peach-Pineapple Frappé. Prepare as above, but after blending, pour into a glass filled with crushed ice.

GOLDEN DAWN

Illustrated opposite.

This tempting drink is made with a blend of dried pear, pineapple juice and orange juice, topped with a snowy egg white head and drizzled with pure maple syrup.

¾ cup pineapple juice
¼ cup fresh orange juice
2 dried pear halves
Thinly pared strip of orange peel
½ egg white
1 teaspoon pure maple syrup
Small flower

1. Combine the pineapple and orange juices.

2. Soak the dried pears and strip of orange peel in the mixed juices overnight.

3. Discard the strip of orange peel. Pour the fruit and juice into a blender and blend until smooth. (If the consistency is too thick, add a little extra pineapple juice.)

4. Strain the mixture and pour into a tall glass.

5. Whisk the egg white until it stands in soft peaks, then spoon over the liquid.

6. Just before serving, drizzle the maple syrup over the egg white. Garnish with a small flower.

PEACH-VANILLA MILK SHAKE

Dried peaches are blended with vanilla-flavored milk in this delectable milk shake.

2 medium or 3 small dried peaches
1/2 vanilla bean, split lengthwise
1 cup milk
Twist of orange peel

1. Soak the dried peaches and vanilla in the milk overnight.

2. Remove the vanilla bean, place the peaches and milk in a blender and blend until completely smooth.

3. Strain the mixture into a tall glass and garnish with a bright twist of orange peel.

Variation:
Pear Vanilla Milk Shake. Follow the above procedure, substituting 2 dried pear halves for the peaches and garnish with a twist of lemon peel.

PEAR-APPLE COCKTAIL

Dried pear is blended with apple juice in this refreshingly fruity drink.

2 dried pear halves
Thinly pared strip of lemon peel
1 cup apple juice
Small yellow or white flower

1. Soak the dried pear halves and strip of lemon peel in the apple juice overnight.

2. Discard the lemon peel, place the fruit and juice in a blender and blend until completely smooth.

3. Strain the mixture into a tall glass. Garnish with a small yellow or white flower to add some color.

PEAR-LEMON MILK SHAKE

This delectably creamy blend of dried pears and milk has the added tang of fresh lemon juice and lemon zest.

2 dried pear halves
Thinly pared strip of lemon peel
1 cup milk
2 teaspoons fresh lemon juice
Finely grated lemon zest
Twist of lemon peel

1. Soak the dried pears and strip of lemon peel in the milk overnight. (The lemon peel will add flavor to the soaking liquid.)

2. Discard the lemon peel and place the pears and milk in a blender.

3. Add the lemon juice and blend until completely smooth and creamy, adding a little additional milk if the consistency is too thick.

4. Strain the liquid into a tall glass.

5. Sprinkle finely grated lemon zest over the milk shake and garnish with a bright twist of lemon peel.

PINEAPPLE FRAPPE

Dried pineapple is blended with milk, poured over crushed ice and sprinkled with grated orange zest in this cooling, delicious frappé.

6 chunks dried pineapple
Thinly pared strip of orange peel
1 cup milk
Crushed ice
Finely grated orange zest
Twist of orange peel
Small yellow flower

1. Soak the pineapple and strip of orange peel in the milk overnight.
2. Remove the orange peel, place the pineapple and milk in a blender and blend until smooth.
3. Fill a tall glass with crushed ice and strain the liquid over the ice.
4. Sprinkle finely grated orange zest over the frappé and garnish with a twist of orange peel and a small yellow flower.

SEVILLE

Sweet dried apricots are blended with orange juice and passion fruit in this delicately fragrant cocktail.

3 medium or 4 small dried apricots
1 cup fresh orange juice
1/2 passion fruit
Twist of orange peel
Small flower

1. Place the dried apricots in the orange juice.
2. Scoop out the seedy pulp from the passion fruit, add to the apricot-orange juice mixture and soak overnight.
3. Strain the juice into a blender and add the soaked apricots. Press the passion fruit seeds remaining in the sieve with the back of a spoon, so that all the fragrant juice is extracted. Discard the seeds.
4. Blend the mixture until it is completely smooth.

5. Strain the liquid into a tall glass and garnish with a twist of orange peel and a small, brightly-colored flower.

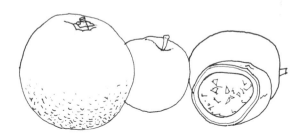

SHANGRI-LA

This colorfully exotic cocktail is a blend of dried apricots and orange juice, capped with a mound of snowy egg white, drizzled with a deep-red raspberry and honey purée.

3 medium or 4 small dried apricots
Thinly pared strip of orange peel
1 cupful fresh orange juice
2 tablespoons raspberries, hulled and rinsed
1/2 teaspoonful clear honey
1/2 egg white
Small flower

1. Soak the dried apricots and orange peel in the orange juice overnight.

2. Discard the orange peel, place the fruit and juice in a blender and blend until completely smooth. Strain.

3. Press the raspberries through a nylon sieve to purée. Add the honey and blend well so that the honey is thoroughly absorbed.

4. Whisk the egg white until it stands in soft peaks.

5. Pour the apricot-orange juice mixture into a tall glass. Pile the egg white over the blended juices, then drizzle the raspberry-honey purée over the egg white.

6. Garnish with a small, exotic-looking flower and serve accompanied by an iced-tea spoon.

Note: Use frozen raspberries if fresh ones are unavailable.

TAHITIAN WEDDING

Dried papaya is blended with milk, veiled with snowy folds of egg white and topped with a strawberry and honey purée in this colorful, mouth-watering cocktail.

⅓ cup dried papaya
2 unblanched, whole almonds, split
1 cup milk
½ egg white
2 strawberries, hulled and rinsed
½ teaspoon clear honey
Small flower

1. Soak the dried papaya and almonds in the milk overnight.

2. Remove the almonds, place the papaya and milk in a blender and blend until smooth. Strain and pour into a tall glass.

3. Whisk the egg white until it stands in soft peaks, then spoon over the drink, allowing the egg white to float on top.

4. Press the strawberries through a nylon sieve to purée. Add the honey and blend well so that the honey is thoroughly absorbed.

5. Drizzle the strawberry-honey purée over the egg white just before serving and garnish with a small, exotic-looking flower. Serve accompanied by an iced-tea spoon.

Note: Use frozen strawberries if fresh ones are unavailable.

3.
FLAVORED MILKS

ALMOND MILK

¾ cupful unblanched almonds
2½ cups milk

1. Blanch the almonds in boiling water to loosen the skins, then peel.
2. Pound the skinned nuts, using a pestle and mortar, until finely ground. Place the ground almonds in a bowl.
3. Scald the milk, then pour onto the almonds.
4. Cover and leave to infuse for 1½-2 hours, stirring from time to time to disperse the almonds.
5. Strain the almond-flavored milk through a piece of muslin or cheesecloth, taking up the cloth with your hands and squeezing tightly so that all the milk is extracted. Discard almonds.
6. Chill almond milk until ready to use.

Note: Almond milk may also be prepared with ground almonds, although the end result will not be as flavorful. Almond milk makes a really delicious base for fresh fruit drinks, blending particularly well with apricots, nectarines, peaches and pears.

COCONUT MILK

1 fresh coconut
2 cups boiling water

1. Pierce the eyes of the coconut and extract the liquid inside. Reserve.
2. Place the coconut on a hard surface, eye end down and crack open with a hammer. Remove the meat from the shell and coarsely grate. (There is no need to remove the brown skin from the white meat when making coconut milk or cream.)
3. Place the grated coconut meat in a deep bowl and pour the reserved extracted liquid on top. Add the boiling water and leave to infuse for about 1 hour.
4. Strain the coconut-flavored milk through a piece of muslin or cheesecloth, taking up the cloth with your hands and squeezing tightly so that all the milk is extracted. Discard coconut meat.

5. Chill coconut milk until ready to use.

Note: For a less rich-flavored milk, increase the quantity of boiling water in which the coconut meat is left to infuse. Coconut milk may also be prepared by infusing the grated coconut in scalded cow's milk, if preferred.

COCONUT CREAM

Prepare as above and leave to infuse overnight. The cream will separate and rise to the top. Skim the cream from the milk and refrigerate until required. Serve with desserts or in fruit drinks.

OAT MILK

2½ cups whole or skim milk
3 tablespoons rolled oats
Honey or raw cane sugar (optional)

1. Place the milk and oats in a saucepan and bring slowly to the boil.

2. Lower the heat and simmer for 2-3 minutes, stirring all the time, as the mixture thickens.

3. Remove from the heat and leave to cool.

4. Pour the cooled milk-oat mixture into a blender and blend until completely smooth. If the mixture is too thick, thin with a little additional milk.

5. Strain the oat milk through a nylon sieve and sweeten, if you wish, with a little honey or sugar.

6. Chill the oat milk until required.

SOY MILK

½ cup dry soybeans
5 cups water
Cinnamon stick or split vanilla bean (optional)

1. Place the dry soy beans in sufficient water to cover them well and leave to soak overnight.
2. Discard the water and rinse the beans in a colander.
3. Place the soaked beans in a blender with 5 cups of water and blend into a creamy-white mixture.
4. Spoon the contents of the blender into a saucepan and bring slowly to the boil. Lower the heat and simmer gently for about 25 minutes, adding the cinnamon stick or vanilla to flavor the milk if you wish.
5. Strain the soy milk through a piece of muslin or cheesecloth, taking up the cloth with your hands and squeezing tightly so that all the milk is extracted from the pulp.
6. Chill the soy milk until required.

VANILLA MILK

1 vanilla bean, split lengthwise
2½ cups milk

1. Place the milk and vanilla in a saucepan and heat to the boiling point.
2. Remove from the heat, cover with a lid and leave to cool.
3. When the milk has cooled, place in the refrigerator to infuse for at least 2 hours, or until required. The longer the vanilla is left in the milk, the stronger the resultant flavor will be.

Note: When preparing Vanilla Milk, you may use regular cow's milk, skim milk or soy milk. It makes a delicious base for fresh fruit drinks, particularly if the vanilla is left to infuse overnight, causing the milk to be lusciously rich in vanilla flavor.

INDEX